How to FORGIVE THE ONE
who hurt you most of all

— A Life Guide —

How to FORGIVE THE ONE

who hurt you most of all

— A Life Guide —

Created by

DR. SUZANNE GELB, PhD, JD

FIRST EDITION

All rights reserved. This book or any portion thereof may not be reproduced or used in any manner whatsoever without the express written permission of the publisher except for the use of brief quotations in a book review.

Copyright © 2019 Dr. Suzanne J. Gelb, Ph.D., J.D.

Manufactured in the United States of America.

ISBN-13: 978-1-950764-11-2
ISBN-10: 1-950764-11-7

www.DrSuzanneGelb.com

PRAISE FOR... THE LIFE GUIDES

I wrote this life guide on how to forgive the one who hurt you most of all, as well as 10 other life guides on various topics, to help readers successfully navigate some of life's trickiest challenges.

Each Life Guide includes educational information sourced from my three+ decades of coaching and counseling in the field of emotional wellness.

What Readers Are Saying

"I was quite excited to receive your Forgiveness Life Guide and hoped it would help me in healing a particularly intense issue I've been harboring for many years.

So far, nothing has worked and I was beyond ready to get this poison out of my life.

This past weekend, I read and thoroughly completed your guide. It was a definite "Aha moment" for me.

I felt a tangible, immediate shift in my thinking.

This is no joke nor is it an exaggeration but I now feel more energy, clarity, and excitement than I've felt in ages. (think puppy after a bath)

And I'm no longer afraid that the feelings of betrayal might be triggered and resurface because I know I have your guide to get me right back on track.

It was so simple and yet so powerful. I can't begin to thank you enough."

—Beth

"I didn't want to let go of my grudge against my dad, but holding onto it was stressful. This Guide helped me to understand that letting go of my grudge and being forgiving was for ME, not necessarily for my dad. That was liberating.

Dr. Gelb's Guide also helped me stop denying & ignoring my feelings. By feeling, instead of pushing my feelings down (only to later come back up), I felt in charge—instead of somehow controlled by—my feelings."

—Dave

"This Guide lifted the weight of the world from my shoulders.

I was consumed by my anger towards my ex ... until I read this guide. Now I have released my anger (safely,) and I'm at peace. I am so grateful to you."

—Terry

"This guidebook has shown me the difference between natural, healthy, appropriate anger ... and the heavy weight of a grudge. I'm glad that now I know the difference."

—Alexandra Franzen, Published Author, Writing Teacher

"Learning how to love yourself and treat yourself kindly — even when your life, career, body, and relationships aren't 'totally perfect' — is one of the hardest things to do.

Dr. Suzanne Gelb breaks down the art of self-love into practical steps. No woo-woo vagueness. Just easy-to-follow exercises pulled from her 28-year career in the field.

If you're looking for practicality and effectiveness, these Life Guides are a steal of a deal."

—Susan Hyatt, Master Certified Life Coach, Published Author

"Dr. Gelb has a gentle spirit that instantly makes you feel like you've come home. The depth of her wisdom is undeniable, her curiosity is insatiable and her love is palpable. These qualities make her the perfect guide for life.

In the pages of the Life Guides you will find practical and proven processes to support you in living your great life.

Whether it's heart-centered wisdom on navigating the dating world, love-based strategies for becoming a parent, or reaching your ideal weight through kindness, Dr. Gelb's Life Guides are gifts to be treasured."

—Dr. Gemma Stone, psychologist

CONTENTS

Disclaimer   xv

INTRODUCTION

Setting Yourself Free From Anger, Pain and Bitterness.   1

WHAT'S INSIDE AND HOW TO USE THIS GUIDE   15

STEP 1

Understand Why "Grudges" Happen.   16

STEP 2

Write Down Your Feelings.   22

STEP 3

Release Negative Feelings ... Safely.   27

STEP 4

Release Repressed Feelings ... Safely, and Rewrite the Script From the Past.   36

STEP 5

Forgive Yourself.   41

STEP 6

Repair Your Relationship ... With The One Who You
Feel Hurt By.   43

STEP 7

Repair Your Relationships ... With Everyone Else.   50

STEP 8

Prevention and Problem-Solving.   53

STEP 9

Be a Ripple of Love.   63

A FEW FINAL WORDS   70

MORE TIPS, MORE TOOLS

FAQs About Anger, Heartache and Betrayal.   71

WHAT'S NEXT?

Resources… to Keep Learning and Growing.   86

ABOUT THE AUTHOR   95

OTHER BOOKS BY THE AUTHOR   96

INDEX   98

DISCLAIMER

This book is a tool that can help you to learn to forgive the one who you feel most hurt by.

This book contains educational exercises and tips drawn from the author's career in the field of emotional wellness with over 30 years of experience. This book is for informational purposes only, and is not intended to diagnose or treat any illness, nor is it a substitute for professional or psychological advice, diagnosis, or treatment. Always consult a qualified health care professional before engaging in any new, self-help resource (such as this one) and with questions you may have about your health and wellbeing.

Any case material that may be alluded to in this book, including in articles, or in interviews [see Resources section] does not constitute guarantees of similar outcomes for the reader. No results can be promised, since everyone's personal development path is unique. Names and details have been changed for privacy.

Links inside this book to external websites are for informational purposes only. Linking does not imply endorsement of or affiliation with that site, its content, or any product or service it may offer.

All link URLs in this book are current at the time of printing. Link URLs may fail at some point if the page has been deleted or moved. The author and publisher assume no responsibility or liability for broken links.

This concludes the disclaimer portion of this book.

Thank you.

INTRODUCTION

Setting yourself free from anger, pain and bitterness.

Welcome to the Life Guide on How To Forgive the One Who Hurt You Most of all.

If you picked up a copy of this Guide, chances are, you might be feeling ...

- **Wounded.**

    ("I never knew I could be hurt this deeply. What he did is unforgivable.")

- **Angry.**

    ("I can't believe she did this to me! I trusted her!")

- **Angry** ... at yourself.

("I can't believe I'm still upset about this! Why can't I just let it go, already?")

- **Tired**.

("I'm sick of carrying around all this baggage. I know it's time to let go. But every time I try, the anger just comes rushing back.")

- **Broken**.

("Because of what he did, I'm not sure I can ever truly love again. I'm a hopeless case.")

- **Afraid to connect**.

("I'm too vulnerable. I don't trust people anymore. I can't bear to go through this all over again.")

When we feel like we've been mistreated, it is natural to feel hurt.

But…

When we cling to anger and bitterness about what another person said or did, the person we're actually mistreating is ourself.

This negativity can:

- **drain our energy**

and

- **impair the choices we make in relationships.**

It's important to:

— **release the "grudge"**...

whether the person we're upset with is still in our life, or not.

It's important that we:

— **resolve these negative feelings**.

It's important that we:

— **do this for ourselves**...

and

— **learn how to finally let it all go**.

Why the title of this Life Guide ... isn't quite right.

It was quite a challenge to decide what to name this particular Life Guide, because the phrase "how to forgive the one who hurt you most of all" isn't quite accurate.

Why?

Because...

No one has the power to "hurt" you, emotionally.

Yes, people can do things that are:

— "so wrong",

— heart-breaking

and

— seemingly unforgivable,

but...

They don't have the power to:

— "inflict" a particular feeling on you

or to:

— "make" you hold onto that feeling.

You can <u>choose</u>:

- **How you feel in response to someone's behavior.**

You can <u>choose</u>:

- **Whether you hold onto emotional pain.**

Or,

- **Let it go.**

This may sound illogical, but it's quite true.

I'll explain a bit more, because for the practices in this Life Guide to be as effective as possible for you, it's important that this concept is clear.

1. No one can hurt you emotionally.

People can harm you physically, but not emotionally.

When people say,

"You hurt me"

or

"You hurt my feelings,"

that's actually inaccurate and can foster blame.

It's more accurate to say:

"I feel hurt by what you did."

No blame there, just taking responsibility for how you're feeling about someone's actions.

2. You have more power than you think.

When someone does something that:

— "hurts" our feelings

or is:

— deeply wrong

(i.e., *"This is not OK"*),

our natural inclination would be to want to **stop the negative behavior**.

This is **"natural anger"**, and it serves a very important purpose: to bring about change. To **prompt us to take corrective action**.

How exactly does natural anger work?

If we experience something **"that is not OK"** or that we want to **change**, our body often responds with a rush of adrenaline — just the right amount to support us in **taking appropriate corrective action**.

Example:

Your internet connection is down.

"This is not OK. I must get this fixed!"

You feel a rush of adrenaline, which fuels you to call your internet service provider.

That's natural anger in action.

With natural anger, the aggressive (corrective) action is in proportion to a situation — talking calmly to your internet service provider (not yelling about your down connection).

Even though you're frustrated, **you choose to remain calm**.

You choose how you feel.

And afterwards?

You have **another opportunity to choose how you want to feel**.

You get to choose whether you:

— **stay mad** that you couldn't connect to the internet for a certain period of time,

and

— **keep feeding the anger**, storing it up, letting it fester inside ...

or **you can choose**:

— to **let it go**.

3. There are consequences for every action.

If someone does something "wrong," it's appropriate to take corrective action based on what they did.

Examples:

— Leave a spouse who continues to be unfaithful;

— Ground a child who violates curfew;

— Call the police to report a crime.

But…

"Taking corrective action" is not the same as "holding onto a grudge."

There are consequences for inappropriate behavior or misbehavior. But those "consequences" do not have to include holding onto:

— anger,

— grief

and

—fear.

Storing these emotions inside yourself is likely to block you from making loving (and self-loving) choices in the future.

This Life Guide is titled:

How To Forgive The One Who Hurt You Most Of All.

But for all of the reasons I've just listed, a more accurate title might be:

How To Forgive The One Who You Feel Hurt You Most Of All.

Because…

— They didn't "make" you feel hurt.

— You chose to feel that way.

Knowing this doesn't (and isn't intended to) minimize how hurt you feel, but it might help you recognize that how you feel is up to you.

"But Dr. Gelb ... I think you don't understand. I'm not just talking about 'misbehavior' here.

What they did was truly unforgivable. It's not possible for me to simply 'choose' a different emotion."

Forgiving someone does not mean that:

- **what that person did was "OK"**

or that:

- **it's forgotten (like it never happened)**

or that:

- **you should instantly trust them again.**

As I mentioned a moment ago, there are situations where taking **"corrective action"** (which might include ending the relationship) is **perfectly appropriate**.

Forgiveness and corrective action are not mutually exclusive.

— You can choose to forgive someone

AND

— Choose to remove them from your life

OR

— Choose to keep them in your life.

Again:

Choosing to forgive does not necessarily mean that what that person did was "OK."

It means that:

you are choosing to release the anger and pain that you've been carrying around, like a heavy load of baggage.

Because...

you deserve to live a life that's free from those kinds of burdens.

Forgiveness is first and foremost for you.

"No, no. You don't understand. I don't think I explained myself well enough....

It was really, really bad."

I do understand. Sometimes, people do things that are really, really horrendous.

Even then, **it is possible to forgive**.

There's a brave Jewish woman who survived the Holocaust, and later started a small business in the United States.

A few years down the road, her business was set aflame by anti-Semitic vandals, in the dead of night — people committing a hate crime against a woman they barely knew.

On a National Public Radio broadcast in the U.S., a reporter asked this woman,

"How did you manage to forgive all of those terrible people who wronged you, time and time again?"

She said, simply:

*"I did not forgive them ... for them. **I forgave them ... for me.**"*

This woman understands **the true power of forgiveness**.

When you stop clinging to:

- **anger,**

- **pain**

and

- **bitterness,**

you set yourself free.

It is one of the greatest gifts that you can give to yourself ...

to the people that you love ... to your community ...

and to the world.

This Life Guide is intended to help you forgive the one who you feel hurt by, most of all.

That person might be:

— one of your parents,

or

— both of your parents,

your:

— previous partner,

or your:

— current partner,

— a lover from many years ago,

— a friend or colleague at work,

your:

— child,

or your:

— mother-in-law ...

or

— anyone at all.

The principles in this guide can help you to **release the hurt,** no matter who that person may be.

The fact that you purchased this Life Guide indicates that **you are ready to begin**.

You're tired of holding onto the pain — and you want to clear it away.

So, let's begin.

What's Inside and How To Use This Guide.

Inside this Life Guide, you'll find a series of lessons that can help you understand:

— **How "grudges" are formed** ...

— **Why it's healthy and necessary to forgive** ...

— **How to release the negative emotions that are holding you back from having the life that you want** ...

and

— **How to begin repairing relationships with people that your anger has impacted.**

As Alexandra Franzen, my writing coach and friend, told me after reading this guide:

"This guidebook has shown me the difference between natural, healthy, appropriate anger ... and the heavy weight of a grudge. I'm glad that now I know the difference."

The Contents page of this Life Guide gave you a peek at what's ahead.

STEP 1

Understand why "grudges" happen.

People cling to hurtful memories for many reasons.

In spending hundreds of hours with clients, over the past 3+ decades, I've identified **7 typical reasons why "grudges" form ... and stick**.

1. Wanting an apology.

"I won't stop being resentful until Brian apologizes."

2. Self-protection.

"If I stay bitter and keep people at a distance, nobody can hurt me again."

3. Revenge.

"If I forgive Sarah now, I'd be letting her off too easily.

She needs to feel pain, just like I did."

4. Denial.

"I've done absolutely nothing wrong.

This whole situation is totally my mother's fault."

5. Attention.

"When I complain about what my wife did, all of my buddies commiserate with me.

They sympathize with me for putting up with that mean hag, and it temporarily makes me feel better."

6. Identity.

"This pain is part of my story, my life, my identity.

If I let it go ... then who am I?"

7. Repressed emotions.

This can happen when you've experienced other emotional "hurts" in the past, but…

— you **swallowed your feelings**,

instead of…

— **releasing them** (safely).

Those feelings have **resurfaced** and are attached to the grudge you're feeling now, cause it to be:

— "even more intense"

and

— difficult to let go of.

You might have one reason for holding onto a grudge — or several.

Why are YOU holding onto a grudge?

Did one (or more) of those 7 reasons leap out at you, immediately?

- Highlight

or

- Circle

or

- Jot down on a piece of paper…

the reasons that feel true for you.

Then read the accompanying statements that follow, out loud.

1. Wanting an apology.

I could wait 100 years and never receive the "exact" apology that I want to hear.

(In fact, I will never hear the "perfect apology" because the other person can't heal me. Only I can do that.)

I feel that I deserve an apology, but that doesn't justify continuing to harbor all this anger.

All that does is weigh me down, emotionally, and breed negativity in my relationships.

Whether I receive an apology or not, I'm going to find a way to release and resolve the anger that I've been harboring. I owe that to myself.

I owe it to myself to take better care of myself emotionally.

I can learn to do that, for myself.

2. Self-protection.

I don't need to protect myself from feeling hurt again.

I can learn to feel secure within myself, trusting that I can take care of myself, always, no matter what.

3. Revenge.

My need for revenge reflects my own pain and anger.

I don't need to create pain for anyone else in order for me to feel better.

4. Denial.

I am ready to acknowledge how I may have contributed to the situation that I feel hurt me. I would like to forgive myself, too.

5. Attention.

I will no longer complain (or be in pain) in order to get attention from others.

I can give myself the love, connection and attention I'm seeking.

6. Identity.

I am ready to become my true self — someone who is pain-free and at peace.

7. Repressed emotions.

If repressed emotions are fueling my grudge, I can learn how to resolve and release them, fully.

I'm worth it.

I can give that gift to myself.
Reading those statements out loud might make you feel a bit better, at least **for a moment**.

That's wonderful — but know that "affirmations" like these can only provide **a temporary form of relief**, at best.

There's still more work to be done.

Next:

Let's look at the **negative feelings** you've been holding onto, in more depth, and **put them into words** ...

— **Your words**.

So that soon ...

— You can **fully release them**.

STEP 2

Write down your feelings.

As a psychologist and life coach, I almost always begin my sessions with a simple **emotional "check-in"** to help clients get in touch with their feelings.

Why start there?

Because…

It can be difficult to release the emotions that might be holding you back from experiencing:

- **Forgiveness,**

- **Peace of mind**

and

- **Lasting happiness,**

if…

- **You don't really know which emotions are interfering to begin with.**

Start here, with a **writing exercise** to:

— get all those feelings out.

Try not to:

— Over-think your answers

or

— Worry if they sound:

- "positive"

or

- "negative"

or even

- "irrational."

Let go of any self-criticism.

Just give yourself **permission to express whatever you feel**.

(This is a form of catharsis: a way to release and get relief from strong or repressed feelings.)

If possible, write your answers on a piece of paper, **by hand** — this process tends to slow people down, giving them time to think.

This way, you might find that you're more involved with what you're writing, rather than, as many people do, typing quickly or not always staying focused on what you're writing.

If there is **more than one person you feel hurt by**, you can **repeat the exercise** for each person.

Fill in the blanks:

The person who I feel most hurt by is

_____

I feel hurt by that person because they

_____

_____

_____

When I think about what that person did, I feel

_____

_____

_____

_____

What they did feels totally unforgivable, because

_____

_____

_____

_____

Whenever I see / think about that person, I still feel

_____

_____

_____

_____

I am mad at myself for

_____

_____

_____

_____

Honest expression is powerful.

But writing down what you're feeling is **just the beginning** of the healing process.

From there,

it's important to discharge and release those feelings in a safe, appropriate way.

(This is what you'll learn how to do next, in Step 3.)

By doing this, you can

start to clear out emotional baggage and release the heavy burden you've been carrying.

STEP 3

Release negative feelings ... safely.

Have you ever noticed what very young children do when they're frustrated or need something?

Sitting in their crib, they'll pound their little hands and feet on the mattress, and probably make sounds to express how they feel, and hopefully get their caregiver's attention.

Once the young child is done pounding, he (or she) is calmer — because all that emotional energy has been released!

The following exercise is essentially the child version of "pounding your crib," but adapted for adults.

Based on my research, as well as decades of professional experience, what I've learned, and observed, is that this technique can be **incredibly effective** — more than just about any other form of catharsis (emotional release).

In my experience, this is, hands down, one of the best ways to clear out the:

- **anger**,

- **bitterness**

and the

- **festering reserves of resentment**

that a lot of people cling to.

Here's how it can be done:

1. Tie a knot at one end of a hand towel,

2. Grab a pillow

and

3. Find a private space — like a home office, den, bathroom or garage with a lock on the door.

Then,

4. Pound that pillow with the knotted end of the towel

while

5. Expressing your feelings, out loud.

Remember:

Any feelings that you express during this exercise, must **only** be directed towards the pillow that's right in front of you — **not** towards any actual person.

That's because…

the purpose of this exercise is to create an opportunity for you to **discharge your intense, pent-up emotions, safely, appropriately and effectively,** in a way that:

— **doesn't** bring harm to yourself (physically or emotionally)

or to

— anyone else

or to

— the environment.

That's why…

you direct and express any of your pent-up emotions towards an appropriate, inanimate object (e.g., a pillow), **but not towards any actual person or object.**

Example:

It's not appropriate to — out of sheer frustration — punch the door with one's fist… and possibly create a hole in the door [made out of wood], even though this type of situation happens, all too often).

Now… back to the exercise.

First, express your anger, on the pillow, towards the person who you feel hurt by.

[Person's name]

_____

I'm so mad at you for

_____

_____

_____

_____

Then, if it feels appropriate for your situation, express any anger (directed at the pillow) that you may be feeling towards yourself:

[Your name]

_____

I'm so mad at you for

_____

_____

_____

_____

Clients often ask me,

"Why would I express anger towards myself?

Isn't that kind of harsh?

Isn't the goal for me to be nice to myself?"

That question is understandable.

Often, when we've chosen to be in relationships with people who mistreat us,

or

we realize how our poor choices have led to the painful situation we're in,

we can be incredibly critical (even mean) towards ourselves.

Angry that we chose that relationship, or those words / actions.

This pounding exercise creates an opportunity for you to discharge any negative emotions that you may be feeling about yourself, safely towards an inanimate object.

This is **far better than letting those feelings fester inside.**

This emotional release is healthy — a kind, loving gesture of self-care from you to yourself.

Keep:

— pounding and repeating,

— pounding and repeating,

— pounding and repeating ...

until you feel a sense of emotional release.

(More on that in a moment.)

"What if it's too noisy? I don't want to scare or disturb anyone!"

You don't have to:

— yell at the top of your lungs

 or

— pound so hard that you build your biceps.

But...

If you're concerned about noise levels, if feasible you can ...

— Turn up the radio or television.

— Make sure that everyone is out of the house, to set your mind at ease.

— Hold a pillow gently up to your face and yell into it.

(Not quite as effective as when combined with pounding, but the pillow muffles sound.)

And / or,

— Have a conversation with the people who share your home, and explain that this pounding exercise is a good thing — a safe, healthy way to release pent-up feelings.

You might even create a designated "venting zone" in your home, where you, and other people in your household, can go whenever there's a need to release pent-up negative emotions.

Again ...

However and wherever you choose to do this pounding exercise, the point is to:

keep expressing how you feel, and keep pounding that pillow, until you feel a sense of emotional relief.

What does "emotional relief" feel like?

When you're done with your pillow-pounding, you might feel:

— a sense of **peace**.

You may find that you want to have:

— a deep, long **cry**.

You might feel:

— quite **drained** — but in a **good** way,

like you've just:

— **unloaded** a heavy **burden**,

and now you're

— experiencing the **fatigue** from having carried that load.

(If that's the case, now's the perfect time to **rest for a bit**.)

These are all **good signs** that you've released some pent-up emotions.

If you're still feeling strong emotions, it doesn't mean that:

— you did the pounding exercise "wrong"

or that:

— it wasn't effective.

It just means that:

There is more emotional energy to release, safely — now, or…you can set these feelings aside until you can create an opportunity to release them safely at another time.

And…

It's possible that it also means that the anger you've been feeling towards someone, is linked to **other past situations** when you felt angry — and **you pushed that anger down**.

Earlier, we talked about:

— **repressed emotions**

(past emotional "hurts" that we swallowed)

as being:

— **one of the reasons that grudges develop.**

Chances are that those repressed feelings have now resurfaced and are fueling your grudge.

That's **why the grudge feels so strong**.

Next, we'll focus on:

- **healing repressed emotions**

and

- **rewriting the script from the past.**

STEP 4

Release repressed feelings ... safely, and rewrite the script from the past.

Our emotions offer us a way to express how we feel.

If something bothers us, for example, it's natural to feel angry.

But when an emotional response is excessive...

For example:

— yelling at the customer service representative, on the phone, when your internet service is down).

or, the emotion lingers...

For example:

— holding a grudge,

this typically means that repressed emotions have surfaced, intensifying our emotional reaction.

It's important to **discharge (cathart) the repressed emotion safely** (like we talked about in Step 3).

Next, try to see if there is a **correlation** between:

- **What you're feeling now**

    (a grudge, for example)

and

- **How you've felt in the past**

    (as far back as you can remember.)

Try asking yourself:

"When have I felt this way before?"

_____

_____

_____

"How old is the part of me that is angry / sad / afraid?"

_____

_____

_____

_____

Accept whatever age comes to mind (even one or two-years-old).

Then ask yourself:

"What does that part of me need?"

Perhaps...

- reassurance,

- understanding

or

- empathy.

Give your inner [fill in the age] __ year-old what he or she needs by **rewriting the script** they learned to live by (and that is still playing in your mind).

This is the script that says,

"I don't deserve..."

or

"I'm not:

- *lovable enough,*
- *good enough,*
- *[fill in the blank] _____ enough".*

Example:

"I'm so sorry that your parents were too busy to pay attention to you.

That was unfair.

But that was then, and this is now.

You deserve *attention and I will give it to you. I am the best parent for you.*

I will never abandon you."

It's so important to understand that our grudge is partly fueled by unrelated "hurts."

Before we can let go of our grudge, those "hurts" must be healed

(by catharting, correlating and rewriting the script).

If those **past hurts:**

— **stay alive**

and

— **remain unattended to,**

they will

— **continue to fuel the grudge** …

and it will

— **continue to stay alive.**

STEP 5

Forgive yourself...

Now that you understand how to let go of a grudge, how are you feeling about yourself?

Are you ready to forgive yourself for holding a grudge?

If the thought of self-forgiveness feels impossible, it probably means that you're still angry at yourself ... and that some more pillow-pounding could be helpful.

That said, **when you're ready to embrace self-forgiveness, try using this script** or something similar:

I forgive you [your name]

for holding onto anger and bitterness.

I forgive you

- *for not knowing how to be free of these negative emotions.*

I forgive you

- *for allowing this negativity to surface in the first place, and to fester.*

I understand.

I love you.

Beautiful.

Now that you have been so kind to yourself, consider (if appropriate) attempting to:

— repair the relationship with the person you feel hurt by.

That's what we'll cover next.

STEP 6

Repair your relationship ... with the one who you feel hurt by.

If the person who you feel hurt by is still a part of your life — if they're your partner, your child, mother-in-law, or a close friend, for example — it's **essential to release the grudge** and **move on**.

Otherwise, your relationship is likely to continue to be burdened by negative emotions.

It's unfair to yourself and to the relationship, if you don't heal the grudge.

When it comes to repairing a relationship, here are a few things to remember:

1. The other person might be holding onto a grudge as well.

When a relationship is in trouble, this is not typically because of **only one** partner's behavior.

To give you an example:

If a husband cheats on his wife, he might seem to be **completely "at fault."**

But **there's a reason why** he cheated.

It might have something to do with his experience with his partner.

— (Maybe his wife was withholding sex or using sex as a bargaining chip.

— Maybe his wife was consumed with work and neglecting the relationship. Or something else.)

This doesn't mean that the husband is "justified" in his behavior or that it's "OK."

But ... it's worth exploring how both people, husband and wife, may have contributed to a scenario that damaged their relationship.

By doing this kind of exploration — which isn't always fun or easy to do! — this relationship is likely to **have a far greater chance of surviving and thriving**.

2. The other person might not be open to repairing the relationship.

Before launching into a discussion about the relationship, it's important to **check in** and see if the other person is **open** to this kind of conversation.

You might say something along these lines:

"I'd like to talk to you about our relationship.

Would you be open to that?"

Or:

"I know I've been keeping my distance, but I'd like to talk to you about our relationship.

Would you be open to that?"

Keep in mind that you've been holding a grudge against them —

which means there's been negativity in the air, and the other person may not be ready, open or receptive to hearing what you have to say.

Talking to them without their consent will be a **waste of energy**.

This could **frustrate** you and cause you to **get angry all over again**, which would make matters worse.

If the other person is not open to discussing the relationship, accept that.

Don't try to:

— manipulate them into saying "yes" to a conversation

(by trying to make them feel guilty if they say "No," for example.)

You have opened the door to having a conversation about the relationship.

You have planted the seed.

They may not be ready to discuss things right now, but they may be **open to talking in the future**.

This is a time for you to be:

- patient

and

- hopeful.

You are healing yourself, and you have attempted to heal your relationship.

You can **feel good** about that.

3. If the other person is open to having a conversation, you could express that:

- **you want to repair the relationship,**

- **you're ready to take responsibility for your anger,**

and, if appropriate:

- **you're ready to take responsibility for the role you played in creating this conflict.**

You can begin by:

— thanking them for being willing to talk.

It's good to open the talk on a **positive note**. This can cause the other person to be **more receptive** to what you have to say.

If it feels right, you can:

— express your love

and then

— state your intent.

You can try using **this script** or something similar:

"Thank you for being willing to talk about our relationship.

I know it may not have seemed like it over these [months, years] but I love you and I really hope that we can heal the rift between us.

I've been very angry at you for a long time.

I've been punishing you for [describe what they did].

_____

_____

_____

_____

What you did was not OK, and it will never be OK.

But I now know that holding onto my bitterness and anger, never letting it go, is not OK either.

It's not healthy or fair to me, and I know that it has been unhealthy for our relationship.

[If it feels appropriate for your situation, you can add:

I also take responsibility for the part that I played in the situation that caused all of this anger.]

I am ready to let go, move on, and rebuild our relationship — hopefully, stronger than ever.

I hope that you are ready, too."

Once you have said those words, give the other person a moment to let it all sink in.

If he or she responds, **listen patiently**.

If he or she chooses not to respond at that time, **let that be OK**.

Don't try to force a conversation.

If you'd like to give that person a hug, ask first:

"Can I give you a hug?"

If he or she is not ready to hug, let that be OK.

Don't try to make it happen.

Or,

If it feels right, just sit quietly for a while, appreciating the beautiful opportunity to share so honestly, and the fresh start you are creating.

Now that you know how to **begin the healing process with the person who you feel hurt by most of all**…

Let's talk about how to repair your relationships with **the other people** who may have been impacted by your anger.

STEP 7

Repair your relationships ... with everyone else.

Holding onto a grudge doesn't just affect you and the person you're angry at.

It can impact **everyone** around you.

— Your kids.

— Your friends.

— Your colleagues.

— Your neighborhood barista, who has overheard you complaining to your friends every Sunday afternoon for the past year ...

You get the idea.

You don't have to "make amends" with everyone, everywhere, but it can be helpful to apologize to the people closest to you.

You could say something along these lines:

"I've been holding a lot of anger towards [person]

Now, I have learned how to release that anger, safely.

I am learning how to forgive, because it is the healthy thing to do.

If you have been impacted by the pain I was holding onto, I am sorry for that.

I know how to manage my emotions more effectively, now.

I'm working to make sure that this kind of situation won't happen again."

The people who are close to you probably don't "need" an apology — but it can't hurt to offer one, anyway.

Make sure, though, that you've forgiven yourself (we talked about this earlier) before you apologize to others.

Why does that matter?

It's important to apologize from a clear, unburdened place.

And of course,

A powerful way to give your apology real weight and meaning ... is to avoid developing a grudge, all over again.

As the American theologian Tryon Edwards once wrote:

"Right actions in the future are the best apologies for bad actions in the past."

STEP 8

Prevention and problem-solving.

When Dave first met Cassie, he thought she was admirably assertive and amazingly confident — unlike any woman he'd ever met.

They married quickly — too quickly — before they really got to know each other.

Soon after they were married, Dave began to see Cassie's true colors.

Less

— "confident"

More

— "self-centered"

and

— "domineering."

Had he discovered this before they married, he probably would have stopped dating her.

But instead, during their marriage, he developed a grudge against her.

"She's insensitive and she never cares about what I think.

She's always bossing me around, and I can't stand it."

His anger only exacerbated Cassie's undesirable qualities. Sensing him pulling away, she became even more:

— controlling

and

— domineering.

Eventually, they ended up in divorce court — unable to let go of their mutual grudges, unwilling to fix their marriage.

In this instance,

years of pain could have been avoided if, while they were dating, Dave and Cassie had realized that they were incompatible

— instead of rushing into marriage during the infatuation stage of their courtship.

That being said, had this couple had the desire to resolve their differences, then it certainly would have been worth pursuing — so that Dave could learn to:

— **let go of his grudge**

and

— step into **being a loving partner**,

and Cassie could:

— **resolve her controlling behavior**

and

— become **more of a team player** and **loving partner**.

That might sound like a pipe-dream, but:

when two people (no matter how incompatible) both have the desire to resolve their issues, the possibilities for personal growth are infinite.

A final comment about the grudge that Dave was holding.

As I often tell my clients:

Anger is a natural emotion.

Its purpose is to bring about change.

If we don't like something, just enough adrenaline is triggered in our body to support the appropriate amount of aggression to bring about a change.

Believe it or not, it takes natural anger to say a healthy "No."

For example:

"No thank you, I'll pass on having more cake."

And, as I also explain to my clients:

It also takes natural anger when we want to take action to change something.

For example:

"My car needs a tune-up. I'll call the mechanic today."

But there's nothing natural about holding onto anger — and allowing it to fester.

Fortunately, this unhealthy habit can be changed.

A good place to start?

1. Self-awareness,

2. Planning

and

3. Problem-solving.

How will you prevent your next grudge from happening?

1. SELF-AWARENESS

First, since grudges develop because we harbor anger about being mistreated, it makes sense to **avoid getting into relationships with people who could mistreat you.**

You could try this script, or something similar, to avoid involvement with a "mistreater."

The next time someone I'm dating does something that raises a red flag, I will stop and ask myself, "Is this the kind of person with whom I want to develop a relationship?"

Your turn.

Complete the following statement.

The next time someone I'm getting to know as a friend or developing a business with, does something that raises a red flag, I will stop and ask myself,

_____

_____

_____

2. PLANNING

Second, since **prevention** also includes **managing your anger** about how someone treated you, next you'll get to **write down**:

— how you plan to manage your anger ...

just like you've learned in this Life Guide.

As a warm-up:

— try this script, or something similar, to manage your anger.

The next time someone does something that rubs me the wrong way, I will manage my anger by pounding a pillow and verbalizing how I feel, until I'm calmer.

Your turn.

Complete the following statement:

The next time I feel hurt, angry or resentful, I will not let those feelings fester inside.

Instead, I will release them safely and appropriately — on the spot, or at the earliest opportunity, by

_____

_____

_____

_____

By filling out these statements, you're writing a little "preventative emotional care plan" for yourself.

You're preparing to manage your emotions — safely and appropriately.

Paying attention and prevention.

You can prevent most injuries at the gym by:

— paying attention to the **physical sensations** in your body,

— **cooling off**

and

— **releasing tension** when you're reaching your limit.

Injuries happen when people **stop paying attention** to their body's signals.

Similarly — and we talked about this just a moment ago, but it's so important, I'll say it again, —

It is possible to nip a potential grudge in the bud by paying attention to your emotions, cooling off and releasing emotional tension, safely, when you feel anger building up inside.

Of course, another way to prevent grudges from forming — or at least, reduce their likelihood — is to be **vigilant** about the experiences and relationships that you choose.

(I mentioned this earlier too, but it's so significant that it's worth repeating.)

If you're choosing to surround yourself with people who frequently do things that feel:

— insensitive,

— uncaring

and even

— emotionally hurtful...

then you appear to be heaping a lot of unnecessary burdens onto your shoulders.

Can you release these emotional burdens?

Yes.

Every time.

But who would want to live like that? That's another question.

May your choices be fueled by:

- **self-respect,**

- **self-worth**

and

- **self-love.**

Why does that matter so much?

Why can that impact the future of our relationships so deeply?

Because:

Then you're not likely to be drawn to negative situations that could be button-pushers — such as

- **dating (or marrying) someone who's incompatible with you,**

or

- **spending a weekend with a relative whose worldview is offensive to you.**

Know that:

— you have the power to release your anger safely, every time, but also take time to ask:

— *"Do I really need this person / this trigger in my life?"*

Maybe you don't.

And that is OK.

When it comes to relationships, **repair** the ones that you want to keep.

And when it's possible, **release** the ones that you don't.

STEP 9

Be a ripple of love.

Now that you've taken steps towards forgiving yourself and the one who you felt most hurt by, you might be feeling ...

- Lighter.
- Happier.
- More hopeful.
- Renewed.

You might also be:

— feeling excited about the new ideas, approaches and tools you've learned.

You might even:

— want to share some of these tools with others who you know.

That's wonderful!

I'm proud and honored to be a psychologist and a life coach, but you don't necessarily have to be an emotional health professional, or expert, to support someone in starting to release a grudge.

If you:

— sense that a friend or a loved one might be holding onto a grudge,

and you'd like to:

— support them,

first ask for:

— permission from them to comment on their behavior.

You could word you request along these lines, or something similar:

"Seems like something's really bothering you.

I'd like to help.

May I share my thoughts about this with you?"

If you get their OK, you could say this or something similar:

"Thank you for allowing me to share my thoughts with you.

I get the sense that you're very angry with [person's name] about [describe the situation],

_____

_____

_____

_____

and I get the sense that this anger is making you feel [sick / sad / heavy / exhausted / hopeless / insert negative emotion (s) here].

_____

_____

_____

_____

Don't get me wrong, I'm not saying that what [person] did was acceptable, but ...

Have you considered what it could feel like to forgive?

If I were in your position, I imagine that releasing all of that anger and heaviness could feel ... amazing.

It could feel like a gift from myself, to myself.

It could feel like freedom."

See what your friend or loved one has to say.

If they are **open** to the idea of forgiveness, you can continue the conversation, and **share your own journey**.

You might want to **make a few notes about your own journey** ... not for the purposes of scripting what you might say, but because it's an emotional subject for you, and therefore, it's easy to get :

— somewhat longwinded

and / or

— side-tracked

when sharing one's own journey with others.

So the purpose of you making a few notes would be to:

— **organize your thoughts**

so that if you have the opportunity to share these thoughts with someone else, it will be easy for them to:

— **understand**

and to

— **grasp how you learned to forgive**,

and how

— **helpful** that was to **you**,

and how

— **helpful** it could be for **them**.

But even if your friend or loved one is not receptive to forgiveness right now, (which means that you won't share your journey with them), it's still a good idea to take a few moments to jot down some notes about your own journey.

Why?

Because learning and growing is an ongoing process, and...

this type of **journal writing** can be a valuable healing and personal growth tool, as you put your journey about **how you found your way to forgiveness**, into words.

Many people find that writing in their journal is like talking to an unconditionally **accepting, non-critical** friend.

With this type of writing there the only rules as that there are no rules — so **disregard spelling** and **punctuation**.

Take as much time and space as you want, to complete your writing.

You can **begin** by filling in the blank lines on the next page, or use your own separate sheet(s) of paper.

After you've **finished writing**, you can read aloud what you wrote. When we read our writing aloud, our appreciation of the words that we wrote is stronger, and reading aloud offers a different perspective.

Then, **continue reading this Life Guide**, beginning after the next page.

WRITING EXERCISE

How I found my way to forgiveness.

_____

_____

_____

_____

_____

_____

_____

_____

_____

_____

_____

_____

Now that you've been so kind and helpful to yourself, by doing the journal writing exercise, here are a few more ways you could, if appropriate, be **be kind** and **helpful to a friend or a loved one** might who be holding onto a **grudge**:

You can:

— Encourage them to seek counseling or coaching, if it appears that they might need that resource.

You can:

— Even purchase another copy of this Life Guide and give it to them, as a gift.

By sharing what you've learned about forgiveness, you can become a ripple of love in the world.

...And here is an article on forgiveness from my archives, that I've shared with the world...

At least 4,400 people liked this article, published on Positively Positive (an online platform with over one million fans):

Still Mad at Your Parents? How to Forgive and Move On, Once and for All.

https://www.positivelypositive.com/2014/08/07/still-mad-at-your-parents-how-to-forgive-and-move-on-once-and-for-all/

A FEW FINAL WORDS

To forgive, is to be strong.

There are very few words that I want to add, to conclude this part of this Life Guide.

I think the following quote sums it up:

"The weak can never forgive. Forgiveness is the attribute of the strong."

— Mahatma Gandhi

That is all.

MORE TIPS, MORE TOOLS

FAQs about anger, heartache and betrayal.

This might seem like an overreach but no matter how hard one is hurting, and no matter what someone did, it is possible to forgive. The choice is yours. Here are even more tips and tools to continue your journey to learn to forgive.

Read on for my answers[1] to some of the more typical questions I've been asked over the past 3+ decades as I've helped people who were feeling cynical, bitter and burdened with heavy grudges, learn to give themselves one of the greatest gifts they could give to themselves — **forgiveness.**

---

[1] Questions and answers have been compiled into general summaries here, to maximize your learning experience.

Question No. 1 — Angry about betrayal

Letting Go of the Need To Know "Why"...

For the past few decades, I have had a very close business partnership with a female colleague. I've invested a lot of time, energy and resources into the business, as has she. Our business has been very successful and rewarding to both of us.

We've also been intimate over the years, and even though we never made a formal commitment to be monogamous, I thought it was an unspoken understanding between us.

I never had any reason to question whether there was anyone else significant in her life, and she never questioned me about that being part of my life, either (she's been the only one in my life since we started being intimate years ago.)

Then, about 7 months ago, I learned, through the grapevine (office gossip), that she was pregnant with someone else's child.

She did not say anything about this to me for the next 2 months, and during that time I was absolutely dumbfounded — both that she is pregnant, and that she hadn't said anything to me about it... and that I had to find out something this personal and this important, basically through water cooler gossip!

When she finally told me, I was defensive and judgmental of what she did. I felt betrayed and angry. This change in circumstances has put a wedge in our personal and professional relationship.

I feel like if I could just understand why she got pregnant with someone else, then I'd be able to stop feeling angry and betrayed. Am I wrong about that?

Response:

I have empathy for your emotional pain.

During my 3+ decades of working in emotional health, I've seen so much heartache and anger, as well as loss and grief because of betrayals.

And all too often, this turns into cynicism and bitterness, and heavy grudges.

But it doesn't have to be this way.

As impossible as it sounds, forgiveness is possible.

Remember:

- **Forgiveness doesn't mean that what the other person did is ok.**

- **Forgiving someone for what they did doesn't mean you're condoning what they did, or will forget about what they did, or saying: "You can do it again."**

- **It means that you let go of your anger that you've been feeling towards them.**

You've been carrying around this burden of anger, and now you're releasing it.

In doing so, you're replacing:

— anger,

— bitterness

and

— hurt,

with

— inner peace.

The question is (and this is also the question that you ask):

— Will **understanding** "why" someone did what they did (e.g., betrayal), resolve the **anger** and sense of betrayal that you **feel** — and that many other people have experienced — when they feel wronged by another person?

The answer, to put it simply and directly, is "No."

Why?

Because although there's no question that it can be helpful to have insight into, and knowledge and understanding of a problem that we're trying to solve, but think about it this way:

In order to understand something, we use our intellect... our <u>mind</u>.

In contrast, however, in this instance, the problem that you're encountering stems from the **emotional pain** that you're experiencing — the **anger** and **sense of betrayal**.

In order to resolve our emotional pain, we need to heal our <u>emotions</u>.

Since "understanding" is connected to our intellect, and not to our emotions, it is not likely that gaining understanding about why your partner did what she did, will offer much healing.

To heal our emotions, they need to be **released**, **safely** and **effectively**.

Otherwise, they're likely to get **backed-up** inside you, and potentially cause physical and additional emotional challenges.

[Note to reader: At this point in my response to this question, I explained how to release anger safely and effectively, using an approach that's similar to the one the you read about earlier in this Life Guide in STEP 3. "Release Negative Feelings ... Safely."]

Keep in mind, as well, that once you resolved all of your anger and hurt using a safe, effective process such as the one I just described, then you can step back and assess the situation using your **intellect**.

Meaning:

Once you've healed your emotions, then, when you "think" about what your partner did, you're able to be more:

— **objective**

and less:

— emotional.

At that point, you may be ready to consider that although you strongly disagree with what your partner did, and how she handled disclosing this to you (she waited for months), she handled it the best way she knew how.

That doesn't mean that:

— she couldn't have done better,

but at that time,

— evidently she did not know how to do better.

Ignorance is not a character flaw. It just means that we haven't learned or mastered something yet. It means we don't know something, yet. It means we haven't learned how to do something better.

That said, ignorance is not an excuse for poor behavior. And, of course, there are consequences for behavior choices.

Keeping the meaning of ignorance in mind, here's a **visualization** that you might want to try:

Choose a private space, preferably a room in your home.

Set aside 5 to 10 minutes where you won't be interupted.

Sit comfortably, or lie down.

Close your eyes.

Take a few deep breaths.

Inhale deeply…

Exhale lightly…

Inhale deeply…

Exhale lightly…

Picture and / or imagine that you're speaking to your partner who betrayed you.

Then visualize yourself saying to her:

"I forgive you for not knowing how to do better."

Remember:

By forgiving your partner, you are lifting your emotional burden of anger and hurt from yourself.

You deserve to do that for yourself.

Question No. 2 — 56 years of hurt

Forgiving my Dad for Being Mean to Me

I'm 56 years old. When I was a kid, my dad was so mean to me.

He wasn't physically abusive or anything like that, but he was always finding fault with me, criticizing me, and putting me down in front of my brothers.

Another mean thing he would do to me was that he would tell me to do things that were way beyond my skill level for my age, and then he would mock me in front of my brothers when I couldn't meet his expectations.

I did well in school because I thought that would please him... but it didn't. He always found something to complain about, when it came to me.

My mom stayed in the background and never stood up for me or came to my defense even though she was aware of my father's meanness towards me.

Later in life, he got cancer. The way things turned out, he ended up coming to live in my home when he was sick, and me and my family took care of him as long as we could, until we needed to put him in a home because he needed more care than we could provide. He passed not long after that.

When he stayed with us, I buried my hurt feelings about how he treated me growing up, but I never ever forgave him, and I'm 56, and I still haven't forgiven him. It feels like if I do, then he got away with everything he did to me, and I'm left feeling angry and hurt. How can that be ok? How can that be fair?

Response:

Thank you for sharing your story about your difficult childhood. That must have been very trying for you. And the emotional scars from those types of experiences in our early years, sometimes take a while to heal.

But rest assured, human beings are amazingly resilient. As such,

There is no emotional scar that cannot be healed.

When it comes to forgiveness though, you might want to ask yourself two questions:

QUESTION 1:

"Who is hurting more right now over how my dad mistreated me when I was growing up?

Me or my dad?"

QUESTION 2:

"Who hurt more when I was a child over how my dad mistreated me during those early years of my life?

Me or my dad?"

The answer to both questions is: *"Me."*

In both instances, YOU are paying the price for holding onto your anger and hurt about your dad being mean to you.

You have every right to feel the way you do, but ask yourself: these next 3 questions:

QUESTION 1:

"Am I being fair to myself by holding on to this hurt?

YES or NO?"

QUESTION 2:

"Am I being fair to myself by subjecting myself as an adult (as you said, you're 56 years old) to same hurt feelings that I felt throughout my childhood when I was a defenseless little child?

YES or NO?"

QUESTION 3:

"Who is benefiting by me holding onto this hurt?

Me or my dad, on NO ONE?"

I imagine you answered *"NO"* to questions 1 and 2, and *"NO ONE"* to question 3. So now you have a better understanding that the right thing to do, **the fair thing to do, for yourself,** would be to begin learning how to **forgive** your father.

That would be **fair** to you. **And that's what matters.**

Question No. 3 — Husband cheated on me

Too Late To Confront, Never Too Late to Heal

My husband died earlier this year. He was 47 (I'm 42). His death was somewhat sudden - heart attack. He didn't have the best of habits (liked to smoke cigarettes and was a social drinker), but overall, day-to-day, he seemed to be fine. I think he was under a lot of stress, and that may have tipped things over the edge.

We were married for over 20 years.

We raised two children, who are in their early 20's still living at home. They're responsible young adults, it's just convenient for them to live at home at this time, as they attend college locally.

My question is about what I learned when I was going through his papers after he died, and taking care of his estate, etc. I'm the Trustee. To cut to the chase, I learned that he was having an affair with a younger woman who he met through his work. It had been going on for at least 3 years...the love notes, etc., that I found, tore my heart out. I had no idea...

I don't know how he could have done this to me... to the kids... to our family. And I'm mad at myself for being so mad... for caring...

At the same time, I wonder things like: What did I do wrong?, why wasn't I enough for him?, should I have lost more weight — should I have taken care of myself better. Now I feel so old and unattractive (that doesn't make sense... I did modeling in my younger days, and still get job offers now and then).

And he's not here, so we can't discuss this! I feel like my self-doubt and resentment is going to last forever. Is there a way out of this?

Response:

I am sorry for your loss, and I appreciate all the deep feelings that are surfacing within you — from resentment to self-doubt, and everything in between.

It's understandable that:

— you would have a lot of questions about what went wrong with your relationship and why, and about what you could have done differently, etc.

It's understandable that:

— you might question your attractiveness, as you are doing...

It's understandable that:

— you might feel old, as you are feeling.

But, yes, there is "a way out of this."

All "of this" can be resolved, once you learn how to release all of your feelings, safely and effectively.

It may take some time to achieve this resolution, as well as the support and assistance of a qualified professional... because you're dealing with a lot. But ...

Keep in mind that:

There is no emotional scar that cannot be healed.

Once the healing has occurred, then:

— **anger** and **resentment** can be replaced

with

— **acceptance** and **self-love**.

And

— **self-doubt** can be replaced

with

— **self-confidence**.

A good place to start with a healing journey where anger, betrayal, resentment and sometimes even self-loathing are bubbling up, is to accept how you feel, without judgment.

You might want to try these two **affirmations**, which you can say aloud or quietly in your mind:

"It's ok to feel all the feelings that I'm feeling.

It's ok not to pretend everything is fine and that I'm not feeling what I'm feeling."

Many people have found that being able to "own" how they feel can get them closer to being ready to discharge their feelings, safely and effectively.

Also, even though your husband has passed, you might want to consider writing some of your feelings down in a **journal**, as if you're talking directly to him.

Make sure that your journal is kept in a secure, private place, so that it is for your eyes only. Then you're likely to feel completely comfortable to express / write what's on your mind.

Think of your journal as a wise, accepting friend who does not judge anything you do or say. This way, your can write down your thoughts and feelings, without feeling a need to edit or censor anything that you express.

In your journal, for example, you might start by expressing the following statements or something similar:

I'm

[fill in the blanks with your feeling/s — angry / hurt / sad, etc]

_____

_____

because you

_____

_____

and I feel so

_____

_____

What you did feels unforgivable and

_____

_____

I just want to

_____

_____

If you feel angry at yourself for whatever reason, you can use these same types of statements to express how you feel — about yourself.

Don't hold back.

Give yourself permission to release as much as possible of what's on your mind and in your heart, on paper.

Self-expression can be a useful first step of forgiveness.

WHAT'S NEXT?

Resources... To Keep Learning and Growing

This Life Guide is "technically" complete, but I wanted to give you some more resources on **self-care** (because when you've felt **emotionally "hurt,"** in some way, in a relationship — and forgiveness hasn't been quite within your grasp yet — **taking exceptional care of yourself is especially important**) ... in case you'd like to continue the learning and the growing with me.

I've included some articles I've authored,[2] books I've written, and inspiring insights that I shared when I was interviewed by a reporter from the Weekend Today Show, for you to browse through when you have time.

---

[2] Except where otherwise noted, all articles referenced in this section were published online.

Self-Care

You Are The Best Investment You'll Ever Make
— Published in Dr. Gelb's column, "All Grown Up" on Psychology Today.

https://www.psychologytoday.com/blog/all-grown/201511/you-are-the-best-investment-youll-ever-make

Why "Certain People" Make Us Feel Completely Insane And How To Reclaim Our "Zen."
— Published on Positively Positive.

https://bit.ly/2HOCdAg

How to Deal With People Who Drive You Absolutely Nuts. (A Life Guide)
— Written by Dr. Suzanne Gelb, Ph.D, J.D.

https://amzn.to/2MzUgi7

Still Mad at Your Parents? How to Forgive and Move On, Once and for All.

https://www.positivelypositive.com/2014/08/07/still-mad-at-your-parents-how-to-forgive-and-move-on-once-and-for-all/

Feeling Phone-verwhelmed? 5 Tips To Help You Create A Healthier, Happier Relationship With Your Smartphone
— Published in Dr. Gelb's column, "All Grown Up," on Psychology Today.

https://www.psychologytoday.com/blog/all-grown/201508/feeling-phone-verwhelmed

Don't Feel Like Exercising? 3 Steps To Get You Off The Couch
— Published in Dr. Gelb's column, "All Grown Up," on Psychology Today.

https://www.psychologytoday.com/blog/all-grown/201505/don-t-feel-exercising-3-steps-get-you-the-couch

Stressed Out at Work? How to Cope -- Without Turning to Food or Booze
— Published on The Huffington Post.

https://www.huffpost.com/entry/stressed-out-at-work-how_n_6711034

The Greatest Cheerleader One Can Have — Lives Within: How To Stay Strong When Not Everyone Is Cheering for our Success.
— Published in Dr. Gelb's column, "All Grown Up" on Psychology Today.

https://www.psychologytoday.com/us/blog/all-grown/201902/the-greatest-cheerleader-person-can-have-lives-within

The Love Tune-Up: How to Amp Up the Love That's Naturally Inside You to Enjoy Happy, Healthy Relationships — A 14-Day Course That Can Change Your Life
— Written by Dr. Suzanne Gelb, Ph.D, J.D.

https://amzn.to/2XQ7190

"Just Believe." How I Learned To Trust In The Universe, Even When All Hope Seemed Lost
— Published in Positively Positive.

http://www.positivelypositive.com/2015/03/26/just-believe-how-i-learned-to-trust-in-the-universe-even-when-all-hope-seemed-lost/

How to Reach Your Ideal Weight Through Kindness, Not Craziness. (A Life Guide)
— Written by Dr. Suzanne Gelb, Ph.D, J.D.

https://amzn.to/2JMqRyi

Welcome Home: Release Addictions and Return to Love
— Written by Dr. Suzanne Gelb, Ph.D, J.D.

https://amzn.to/2vwXmIa

5 Ways to Stop Yourself from Eating When You're not Hungry
— Published on Psych Central.

http://psychcentral.com/blog/archives/2014/10/30/5-ways-to-stop-yourself-from-eating-when-youre-not-hungry/

Learning To Feed My Hungry Heart: My Journey From Bingeing To Wholeness
— Published in Dr. Gelb's column, "All Grown Up" on Psychology Today.

https://www.psychologytoday.com/intl/blog/all-grown/201904/learning-feed-my-hungry-heart

6 Self-Sabotaging Habits You Need To Drop Right Now
— Published on Mind Body Green.

https://www.mindbodygreen.com/0-14014/6-selfsabotaging-habits-you-need-to-drop-right-now.html

If You Want to Make Tomorrow Less Stressful—Start Tonight
— Published in Dr. Gelb's column, "Be Well At Work, on The Muse.

https://www.themuse.com/advice/if-you-want-to-make-tomorrow-less-stressfulstart-tonight

How to Succeed Everywhere: 10 Tips for Balance at Work, Home, in Relationships
— Written by Shelby Marra, published online on NBC's Today.

https://www.today.com/health/how-become-high-achieving-woman-work-your-relationship-parent-t33071

Side note: As my colleague, friend, and gifted writing teacher, Alex Franzen said: *"THIS IS AMAZING! Being interviewed by a reporter from NBC's Today Show? Uh, that's the big leagues!"*

Yes, that's what happened. Shelby Marra with NBC's Today Show in New York, requested an interview with me so that she could write this article featuring me, for TODAY.com's Successful Women series.

How Successful People Do More in 24 Hours Than the Rest of Us Do in a Week
— Published on Newsweek; also published on The Muse.

https://www.newsweek.com/career/how-successful-people-do-more-24-hours-rest-us-do-week

Side note: The Muse is an online platform that attracts more than 75 million people each year, to help them be at the top of their game at work.

I'm honored to have received the praise below, from Adrian Granzella Larssen, Editor-in-Chief, in response to an article that I wrote for The Muse:

"Wow! This is fantastic stuff. You're clearly incredible at what you do, and I'm so thrilled to share your advice with our audience!"

Why Positive Affirmations Don't Always Work (And What Does)
— Published on Tiny Buddha.

http://tinybuddha.com/blog/why-positive-affirmations-dont-always-work-and-what-does/

Why People Resist Seeking Therapy
— Published on Dr. Gelb's column, "All Grown Up" on Psychology Today.

https://www.psychologytoday.com/blog/all-grown/201510/why-people-resist-seeking-therapy

"What Actually Happens During A Therapy Session?"...
And 6 other common questions about psychotherapy
— Published on Dr. Gelb's column, "All Grown Up" on Psychology Today.

https://www.psychologytoday.com/blog/all-grown/201512/what-actually-happens-during-therapy-session

How To Care for Yourself — When You're A Caregiver For Someone Else. (A Life Guide)
— Written by Dr. Suzanne Gelb, Ph.D, J.D.

https://amzn.to/2W1tBKD

Taking Care of an Elderly Parent -- and Not Loving It? How to Turn Resentment Into Patience and Joy
— Published on The Huffington Post.

http://www.huffingtonpost.com/dr-suzanne-gelb/caregiving_b_5260566.html

Ashamed of how you look in a swimsuit? Women: Please Read This
— Published on The Huffington Post.

https://www.huffpost.com/entry/post_n_5541682

Obsessing Over Wrinkles? Depressed About Aging? — 5 Questions To Help You Re-Focus On What Really Matters
— Published in Dr. Gelb's column, "All Grown Up," on Psychology Today.

https://www.psychologytoday.com/blog/all-grown/201502/obsessing-over-wrinkles-depressed-about-aging

Aging With Grace, Strength and Self-Love. (A Life Guide)
— Written by Dr. Suzanne Gelb, Ph.D, J.D.

https://amzn.to/2VYatSx

Had Your Heart Broken? 21 Reasons To Start Dating Again
— Published on Mind Body Green.

http://www.mindbodygreen.com/0-15548/had-your-heart-broken-21-reasons-to-start-dating-again.html

7 Questions To Ask Before You Start A Rebound Relationship
— Published on Mind Body Green.

http://www.mindbodygreen.com/0-17955/7-questions-to-ask-before-you-start-a-rebound-relationship.html

How To Navigate Being Single — And Savor Your Dating Adventure. (A Life Guide)
— Written by Dr. Suzanne Gelb, Ph.D, J.D.

https://amzn.to/2QKm1CS

How to Find Work That You Love When You're Stuck in a Job That You Hate. (A Life Guide)
— Written by Dr. Suzanne Gelb, Ph.D, J.D.

https://amzn.to/2YmrFO2

The Life Guide on How to Rekindle That Spark and Create the Relationship and Sex Life That You Want.
— Written by Dr. Suzanne Gelb, Ph.D, J.D.

http://drsuzannegelb.com/rekindle-spark/

ABOUT THE AUTHOR

Dr. Suzanne Gelb, PhD, JD is a psychologist, life coach and author. For 3+ decades, she has helped people learn to forgive others who have hurt them, and reclaim happiness and wellbeing, using tools like the ones in this book.

Dr. Gelb's inspiring insights on emotional wellness have been featured on more than 200 radio programs, 260 TV interviews, and online on Time, Newsweek, Forbes, Psychology Today, The Huffington Post, NBC's Today, Positively Positive, Mind Body Green, The Muse and many other places, as well.

Dr. Gelb's powerful articles, *Still Mad at Your Parents? How to Forgive and Move On, Once and for All*, and *"Just Believe." How I Learned To Trust In The Universe, Even When All Hope Seemed Lost* were published on Positively Positive. As a contributing writer to Psychology Today, Dr. Gelb's articles on self-healing [so necessary after being emotionally hurt] include *How To Prioritize Self-Care When Life's "Super Busy."*

Dr. Gelb believes it is never too late to become the person — you want to be. Strong. Confident. Calm. Creative. Free of the burdens that have held you back — no matter what happened in the past.

To learn more, visit *DrSuzanneGelb.com*.

OTHER BOOKS BY THE AUTHOR

The Love Tune-Up: How to Amp Up the Love That's Naturally Inside You to Enjoy Happy, Healthy Relationships.

How to Deal With People Who Drive You Absolutely Nuts. (A Life Guide)

How To Care for Yourself — When You're A Caregiver For Someone Else. (A Life Guide)

Welcome Home: Release Addiction and Return to Love.

How to Reach Your Ideal Weight Through Kindness, Not Craziness. (A Life Guide)

How To Navigate Being Single — And Savor Your Dating Adventure. (A Life Guide)

Aging With Grace, Strength and Self-Love. (A Life Guide)

The Life Guide on How to Rekindle That Spark and Create the Relationship and Sex Life That You Want.

Helping Your Teen Make Healthy Choices About Dating and Intimacy. (A Life Guide)

It Starts With You – How To Raise Happy, Successful Children By Becoming the Best Role-Model You Can Possibly Be. A Guidebook For Parents.

How to Get Your Kids to Cooperate and Help Them Become the Best Grown-Ups They Can Be. (A Life Guide)

How To Get Ready To Be a Parent — and Be the Best Mom or Dad You Can Possibly Be. (A Life Guide)

How to Find Work That You Love When You're Stuck in a Job That You Hate. (A Life Guide)

Real Men Don't Vacuum. And Other Misguided Myths That Cause Conflict in Relationships.

INDEX[3]

A

affirmations, 21, 83, 91
afraid to connect, 2
angry (…) at yourself, 1, 41
attention, 17, 20, 27, 39, 59

B

baggage, 2, 11, 26
be(come) a ripple of love, 63, 69
betrayal, 71, 72, 74, 83
bitterness, 1, 2, 12, 28, 42, 48, 73, 90
broken, 2, 93
burdens, 11, 60

C

calm(er), 7, 27, 58, 95
catharsis, 24, 27
consequences, 8, 76
correlation, 37

D

denial, 17, 20

E

emotional baggage, 26
emotional burden(s), 60, 77
emotional "check-in", 22
emotional release, 27, 32
"emotional relief", 33
emotional pain, 5, 73, 74, 75
emotional scar, 79, 83

F

feel hurt by, 6, 13, 24, 30, 42, 43, 49, 63
forgive yourself, 41, 51

H

heal our emotions, 75
how to forgive, 1, 4, 9, 51, 69, 80, 87

---

[3] The page numbers in this index refer to the printed version of this book.

I

identity, 17, 20
it is possible to forgive, 11, 71

J

journal (writing), 67, 69, 84

K

keep learning and growing, 86

L

lasting happiness, 23
let(ing) it go, 2, 5, 8, 17

M

"make amends", 51

N

natural anger, 6, 7, 15, 56
no one can hurt you
   emotionally, 5

P

paying attention, 59

peace of mind, 22
pillow-pounding, 33, 41
pounding exercise, 31, 33, 34
prevention, 53, 58, 59
problem-solving, 53, 57

R

release negative feelings, 27, 75
release pent-up feelings, 33
release repressed feelings, 36
release the "grudge", 3, 43
release the hurt, 14
repair your relationship(s), 43, 49, 50
repair(ing) the relationship, 15, 42, 45, 47
repressed emotions, 18, 20, 35, 37
revenge, 17, 20
rewrite the script from the past, 36
rewriting the script, 35, 38, 40

S

self-care, 32, 86, 87
self-expression, 85
self-love, 61, 83, 93, 96
self-protection, 16, 19
self-respect, 61
self-worth, 61
set(ting) yourself free, 1, 12

T

take/taking corrective action, 6, 8
temporary form of relief, 21
the true power of forgiveness, 12
tired, 2, 14
to forgive, is to be strong, 70
trust, 2, 10, 89

U

use our intellect … our mind, 74
understand why "grudges" happen, 16

V

"venting zone", 57
vigilant, 60

W

wanting an apology, 16, 19
write down your feelings, 22, 84

Y

you can <u>choose</u>, 5, 8, 10

www.ingramcontent.com/pod-product-compliance
Lightning Source LLC
Chambersburg PA
CBHW020143130526
44591CB00030B/195